rodstewartunplugged ...and seated

Photography: Neal Preston

CONTENTS

hot legs

Words and Music by
ROD STEWART

Moderately

Who's that knock-ing on the door, it's got to be a quar-ter to four
Got-ta most per-suas - ive tongue,___ you prom - ise all kinds___ of fun___
- a-gine how my dad - dy felt _____ in your jet black sus-pen-der belt.___

Is it you ___ a - gain, ___ com-ing round for more___
But what you don't un-der - stand ___ I'm a work - ing man ___
Sev - en - teen years old ___ He's touch-ing six - ty four___

Well you can love me to-night_if you want But in the
Gon-na need a shot of vit - a - min E ___ By the
You got ___ legs right up to your neck, You're mak-ing

morn-ing make sure you're gone, ___ I'm talk-in' to you. Hot legs, (you're)
time ___ you're fin-ished with me, ___ I'm talk-in' to you. Hot legs, you're an
me ___ a phys-i-cal wreck, ___ I'm talk-in' to you. Hot legs, in your

wear-ing me out. ___ Hot legs, you can scream and shout, ___
Al-ley Cat, ___ Hot legs, you scratch my back. ___
sat-in shoes, ___ Hot legs, are you still in school, ___

To Coda ✛

Hot legs, are you still in school, ___ I love you honey.
Hot legs, bring your mo-ther too, ___ I love you honey.
Hot legs, you're mak-ing me a fool ___ I love you honey.

Hot legs,

Hot legs,

tonight's the night
(gonna be alright)

Words and Music by
ROD STEWART

handbags and gladrags

By
MICHAEL D'ABO

1. Ev - er seen a blind man cross the road tryin' to make the oth - er side?
2. Once I was a young man, and all I thought I had to do was smile.

cut across shorty

Words and Music by
MARIJOHN WILKIN and
WAYNE WALKER

every picture tells a story

Words and Music by
ROD STEWART and RON WOOD

2. Paris was a place you could hide away, if you felt you didn't fit in.
French police wouldn't give me no peace, they claimed I was a nasty person.
Down along the Left Bank, minding my own, was knocked down by a human stampede;
Got arrested for inciting a peaceful riot, when all I wanted was a cup of tea.
I was accused.

3. I moved on.
Down in Rome I wasn't getting enough of the things that keep a young man alive.
My body stunk, but I kept my funk at a time when I was right out of luck.
Getting desperate, indeed I was looking like a tourist attraction.
Oh, my dear, I better get out of here for the Vatican don't give no sanction.
I wasn't ready for that, no, no.

4. I moved right out East, yeah!
On the Peking ferry I was feeling merry, sailing on my way back here.
I fell in love with a slant-eyed lady by the light of an eastern moon.
Shanghai Lil never used the pill, she claimed that it just ain't natural.
She took me up on deck and bit my neck. Oh, people, I was glad I found her,
Oh, yeah, I was glad I found her.

5. I firmly believed that I didn't need anyone but me.
I sincerely thought I was so complete. Look how wrong you can be.
The women I've known I wouldn't let tie my shoe. They wouldn't give you the time of day,
But the slant-eyed lady knocked me off my feet. God, I was glad I found her.

6. And if they had the words I could tell to you to help you on your way down the road,
I couldn't quote you no Dickens, Shelley or Keats, 'cause it's all been said before.
Make the best out of the bad, just laugh it off.
You didn't have to come here anyway.   So remember: [To final ending]

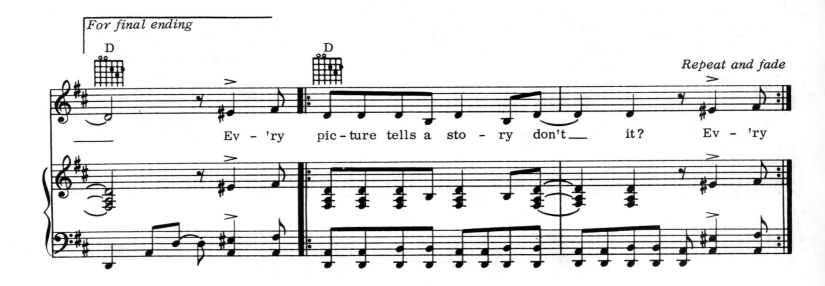

maggie may

Words and Music by
ROD STEWART and
MARTIN QUITTENTON

Medium Rock beat

1.Wake up, Mag-gie, I think I got some-thing to say to you.___ It's late Sep-tem-ber and I real-ly should___ be back___ at___ school.___

what real - ly hurts.

2. The

Repeat and fade

2. The morning sun, when it's in your face,
   Really shows your age.
   But that don't worry me none.
   In my eyes, you're everything.
   I laughed at all of your jokes.
   My love, you didn't need to coax.
   Oh, Maggie, I couldn't have tried any more.
   You led me away from home
   Just to save you from being alone.
   You stole my soul, and that's a pain I can do without.

3. All I needed was a friend
   To lend a guiding hand.
   But you turned into a lover, and, mother, what a lover!
   You wore me out.
   All you did was wreck my bed,
   And, in the morning, kick me in the head.
   Oh, Maggie, I couldn't have tried any more.
   You led me away from home
   'Cause you didn't want to be alone.
   You stole my heart. I couldn't leave you if I tried.

4. I suppose I could collect my books
   And get on back to school.
   Or steal my daddy's cue
   And make a living out of playing pool.
   Or find myself a rock 'n' roll band
   That needs a helping hand.
   Oh, Maggie, I wish I'd never seen your face.
   You made a first-class fool out of me.
   But I'm as blind as a fool can be.
   You stole my heart, but I love you anyway.

reason to believe

Words and Music by
TIM HARDIN

people get ready

Words and Music by
CURTIS MAYFIELD

die - sels hum - ming. Don't need no tick - et, you just thank the Lord. __
doors and board __ them. There's hope for all __ among the loved the most. __

There ain't no room __ for the

hope-less sin - ner __ who would hurt __ all man-kind __ just to save __ his own. __ Have

have i told you lately

Words and Music by
VAN MORRISON

Slowly, with expression

Have I told ___ you late-ly that I love you? Have I

told you there's no one else ___ a-bove ___ you?

Fill my heart ___ with glad-ness, take a-way all ___ my sad-ness,

tom traubert's blues

Words and Music by
TOM WAITS

Verses:

5. No, I don't want your sympathy,
The fugitives say the streets arent for dreaming now.
Manslaughter dragnets and the ghosts that sell memories,
They want a piece of the action anyhow. Go . . . *(Chorus)*

6. And you can ask any sailor,
And the keys from the jailer,
And the old men in wheelchairs know
That Matilda's the defendant, and she killed about a hundred,
And she follows wherever you may go. *(Chorus)*

(𝄋)7. And it's a battered old suitcase to a hotel some place,
And a wound that will never heal.
No prima donna, the perfume is on an old (shirt . . . *etc.*) *To Coda*

the first cut is the deepest

Words and Music by
CAT STEVENS

mandolin wind

Words and Music by
ROD STEWART

Moderate country-rock

When the rain__ came____ I thought you'd leave,_____ 'cause I

knew how much____ you loved the sun; But you

chose to stay,__ stay__ and keep me warm__ through the

2. Oh, the snow fell without a break,
   Buffalo died in the frozen fields, you know.
   Through the coldest winter in almost fourteen years
   I couldn't believe you kept a smile.
   Now I can rest assured, knowing that we've seen the worst,
   And I know I love ya.

3. Oh, I never was good with romantic words,
   So the next few lines come really hard.
   Don't have much, but what I've got is yours,
   Except, of course, my steel guitar.
   Ha, 'cause I know you don't play
   But I'll teach you one day
   Because I love ya.

4. I recall the night we knelt and prayed,
   Noticing your face was thin and pale.
   I found it hard to hide my tears,
   I felt ashamed, I felt I'd let ya down.
   No mandolin wind couldn't change a thing,
   Couldn't change a thing, no, no.

highgate shuffle

Arranged by
ROD STEWART

It was

I said bye, __

bye bye, ba - by, bye bye. __   I said bye, __

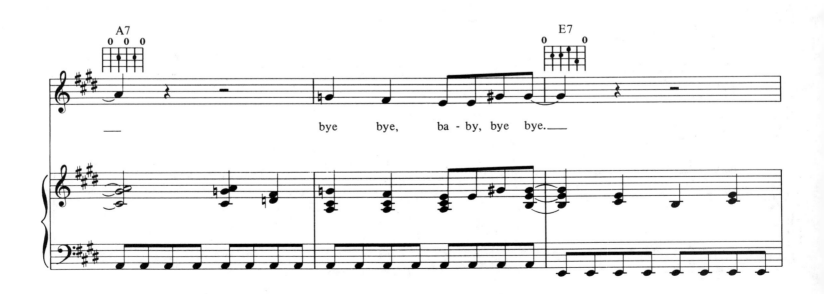

bye bye, ba - by, bye bye. __

stay with me

Words and Music by
RON WOOD and
ROD STEWART

Moderate Rock

In the morn-

in'__ don't say you love __ me 'cause I'll on-

ly kick you out of the door. __ I

know your name _ is Ri - ta   'cause your per-fume's smell-in' sweet - er   since

when I saw you down on the floor. ___

Lead Guitar

You won't

64

having a party

Words and Music by
SAM COOKE